Make Android games within 1 hour.

By: Dennis Saxton

Thank you for purchasing this book. Developing a mobile app isn't as hard as you may think it is. This book was designed to overcome your fears about the difficulties of designing mobile games from scratch.

Construct 2

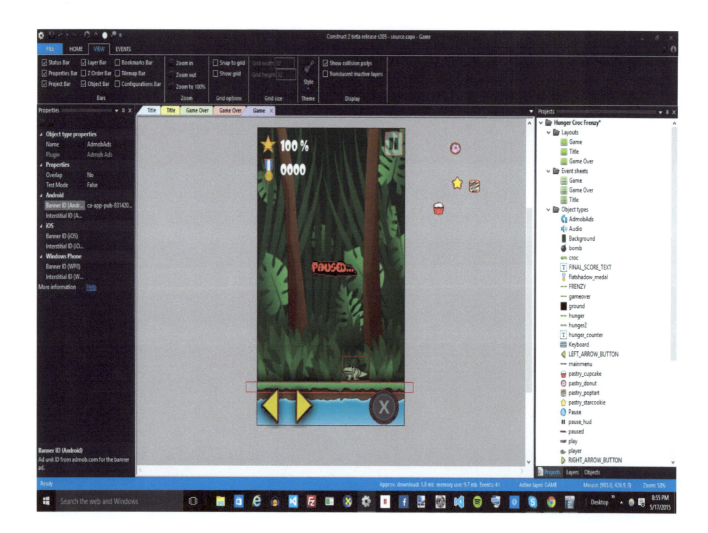

Construct 2 is a high quality game engine that creates HTML5 games. HTML5 allows you to play games on supported web browsers on your desktop, tablets and even your mobile phone. Instead of typing code, Construct 2 simplifies the process by using a "Point and Click" event system and a "Drag and Drop" 2D Editor. In order to export Android games from Construct 2, you will need to purchase their "Personal" Edition License.

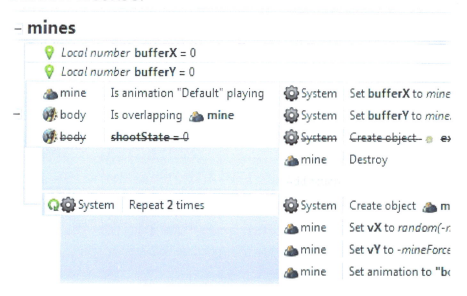

What will we create after going through all the steps in this book?

After reading and applying each step from this book, you will have accomplished creating a mobile game called "Hunger Croc Frenzy." The game's objective consists of simple gameplay which involves controlling an alligator with the left and right touch keys, while making sure that the alligator eats as many snacks as possible before the time runs out.

Let's get started!

You will first need to download Construct 2 from Scirra's website (http://www.scirra.com) It is highly recommended that you purchase the "Personal" Edition which is needed to export projects to Android (Cordova) which we will use to make our mobile game. The Personal Edition is $130 one-time fee.

Next, you will need to download the "Hunger Croc Frenzy" asset pack. This is all the images, music, and plugins we will need to create the game. You can download it now, by clicking the link below or typing it in your favorite web browser. After downloading, then extract the assets folder to any place where you can find the files easily. For the "rex_pause" folder. You will need to extract to (Construct 2 Install Directory\exporters\html5\plugins). View the picture below for help.

Asset Pack Download:
https://dl.dropboxusercontent.com/u/59278223/hungercroc.zip

Thanks to Vicki Wenderlich for the wonderful graphics. These graphics are under a Creative Commons Attribution License. You can get more of her free and paid graphics from http://www.gameartguppy.com.

For further licensing information, you can visit http://www.gameartguppy.com/about/license.

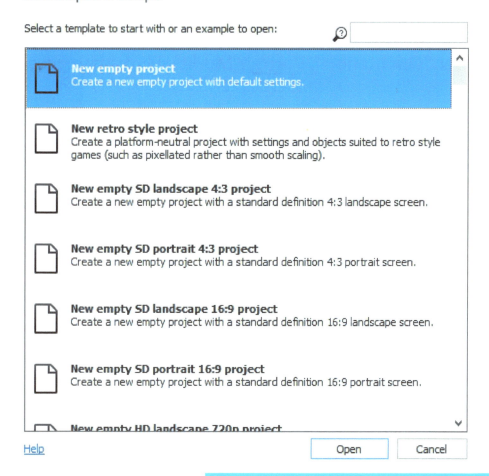

Open Construct 2. Click **File** > **New** > Select **New Empty Project**

Construct 2 will create a new project with a blank white screen which looks like a sheet of paper. Now you will need to change some of the project's properties.

Name: Hunger Croc Frenzy

Version: 1.0 (You would update this number each time you want to update the game)

Description: Any description of your choice.

ID: com.yourcompanyname.hungercrocfrenzy (You need to create a unique name as this will be important for later. If your company name is "Joe's Apps, then your id would be com.joesapps.hungercrocfrenzy)

Author: Your Name

Email: Your Email

Website: Your website

Now you will need to set the Window Size to "640x960". This is an optimal resolution size for Android devices in "Portrait" mode which you need to set under "Orientation". Portrait Mode will display the game horizontally.

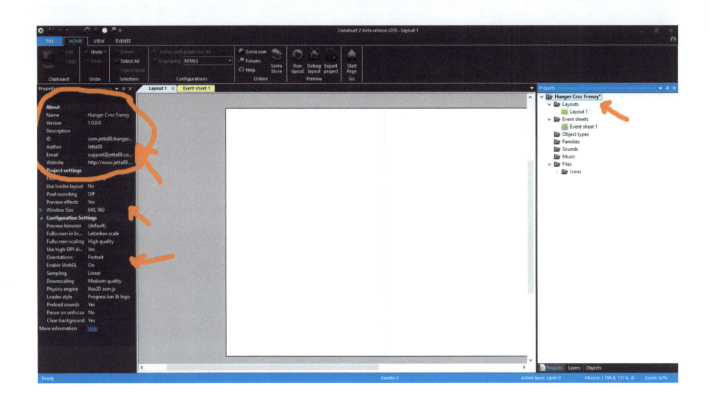

Under Layouts, Right-Click on "Layout 1". Rename this layout to "Main Menu" and then change it's Layout Size to 640,960. This will make the adjust the white layout to match the same size of the project's window size. You will also need to rename the Event Sheet to "Main Menu" as well.

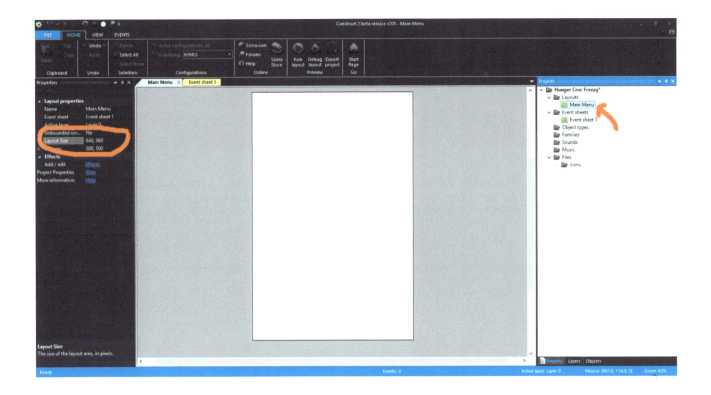

Double-click outside the layout and you will now come across a "Insert New Object" window. Add the Audio object. Next will import our Sound and Music files that's included inside the asset pack. In the Project, find the Sound and Music folders. Right click and then you can import the sound files as shown below.

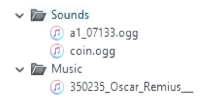

Now double-click outside the layout and you will now come across an "Insert New Object" window. We need to select "Tiled Background." Click anywhere on screen, and then open up "background.png" file from the Hunger Croc Frenzy assets pack folder.

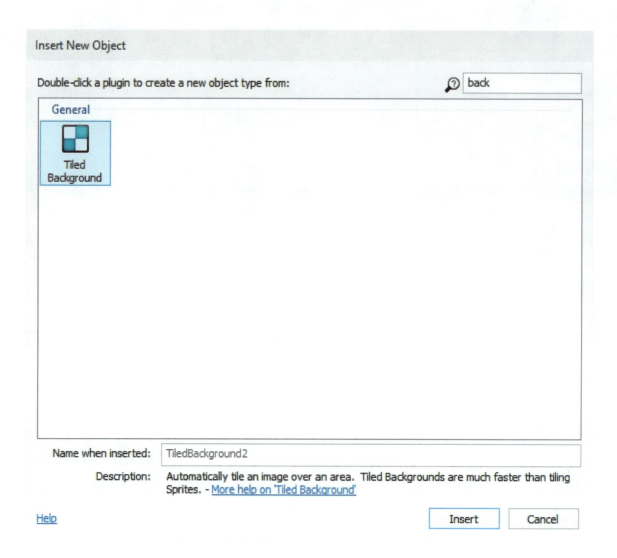

After you've added the background, under "Object Type properties", rename the background as "Background." Change the Position to (0,0) and change the size to 640,960. You will see the background correctly re-position and resize itself on the project's layout.

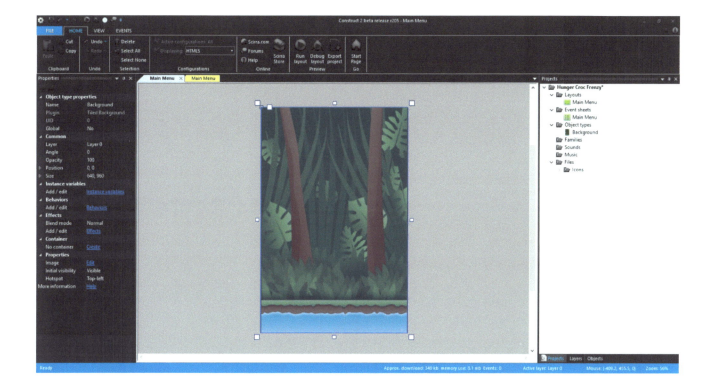

Nice! You now have a background showing instead of a plain white screen. Now go ahead and save your progress by going to *File > Save as Single File*. This will create a .capx file that you can use to open anytime in Construct 2 to continue your progress or add new features in the future.

In the assets folder, drag "Hunger.png", "Croc.png","Frenzy.png" and "play.png" images into the project. After those images are imported into the project, you want to make sure that "play.png" has a perfect box collision. Having a perfect box collision will allow our player to easily select the button on a mobile device. To do this, you will need to double-click on the image.

Drag out the points and delete points that
not really needed by selecting them and
hitting the "Delete" button on your keyboard.

After you position all of the images that you imported, it should look
something similar to this.

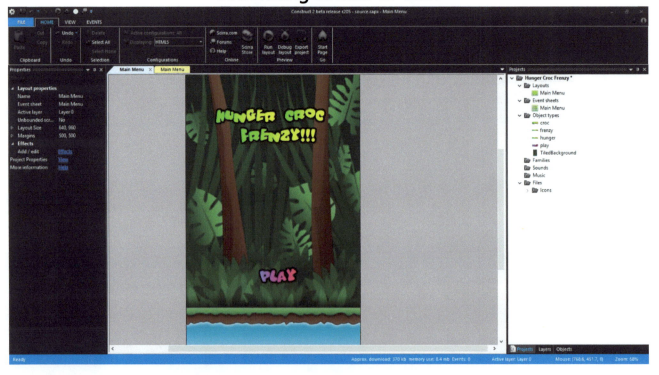

Next Step:

- Save your progress.
- Make a new layout and event sheet called "Game"
- Make 2 layers, "Game" as Layer 0 and "UI" as Layer 1. We need two different layers and you always want the UI layer to come in front of the Game layer, because it's the most important screen. The UI screen will show things like scores, timers, etc.
- Double click outside the "Main Menu" layout from the "Add New Object" window select "Touch". This will enable mobile touch features in the project.
- Now open up the "Main Menu" event sheet. Click on "Add Event".
- Select Touch then select "On Touched Object"
- Choose the "Play" object, then click "Done".
- Click on "Add Action"
- Select "System" and Under "General" select "Go to Layout"
- Make sure "Game" and then click OK. If you successful done all of the steps, it should look like this..

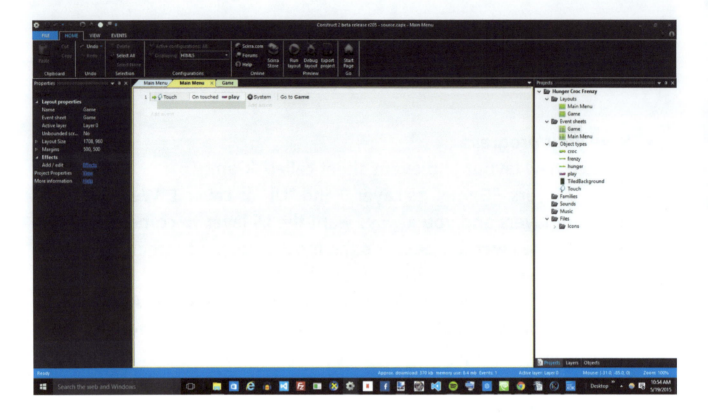

Save your progress and now go back to the project properties. You can now change the the "First Layout" to "Main Menu". This will make the game start at the main menu.

Game Core

We will now start working on the game core. This will be the most important area of the whole game and will require more events than any other layout we've created for this game.

- Open "Game" layout
- Click the "Layers Tab
- Rename "Layer0" to "Background"
- Create a new layer by clicking the "Plus" sign button and rename it to "HUD"

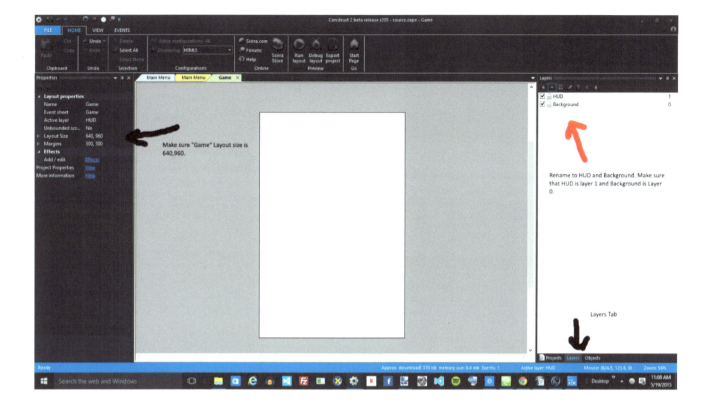

- Under Layout Properties, make sure that the Active Layout is set to "Background"
- Click the "Projects" tab. Rename TiledBackground to "Background" and Drag the Background onto the project.
  - Set the position of the background to (0,0)

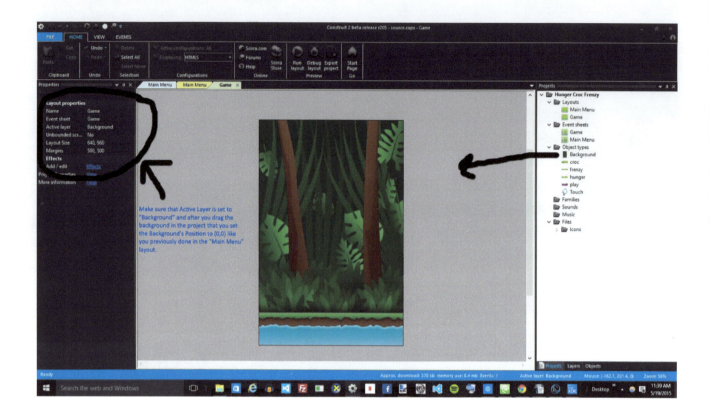

Add the rest of the assets in the project now

First we need to add the PauseNow you need to add the rest of the project graphic assets in the game, by dragging from the folder onto the project, but before you do that. Make sure that the "Active Layer" is set to "HUD"

Drag the following into the project:

pastry_cupcake.png
pastry_donut.png
pastry_poptart.png
pastry_starcookie.png
pausedHUD.png
pausebuttonHUD.png
starHUD.png
medal.png
leftarrow.png
rightarrow.png
xbutton.png

bomb.png

For our food objects "pastry_cupcake, pastry_donut, pastry_poptart and pastry_starcookie", we need to add the Bullet behavior. Bullet behavior is used for custom movement with our objects which will be using for later. To do this, right-click on each object and select "Behaviors". Click the Plus sign and add "Bullet" behavior.

Now we need to adjust our bullet project as follows.

	pastry_cupcake	pastry_donut	pastry_poptart	pastry_starcookie
Speed	0	0	0	0
Acceleration	0	0	0	0
Gravity	50	90	100	175
Bounce off solids	No	No	No	No
Set Angle	No	Yes	Yes	No
Initial state	Enabled	Enabled	Enabled	Enabled

Each object uses a different gravity setting, because it will affect the speed at which each objects fall from the sky when our alligator catches food.

Our last step requires us to add the "Pause" object in our project. You can do that by double-clicking outside our layout and adding the Pause object.

Asset Size and Position Customization

Once you have all of your assets in your project, it's time to re-position them to make your project more like a game. For example, look at the left and right arrows. These two arrows need to be on the left-most area of our layout.

For the left arrow image, set the Position to (65,897) and the Size to (149,147). For the right arrow image, set the Position to (227,897) and the Size to (149,147). You can all of these position edits can be changed under the object properties for each object. After you make those changes, you will see the left and right arrow re-position and re-size on your layout.

You don't have to use these same values, you can also drag and drop the images to where you want on your screen, but it's recommended that you follow the values that I give you to follow along with this book. *Please remember that any images not showing inside the layout, will not show on your game screen.*

Size and Positions for other images	Position	Size
xbutton	X: 558 , Y: 888	X: 148, Y: 128
paused	X: 343 , Y: 453	X: 162 , Y: 45
medal	X: 79 , Y: 215	X: 57 , Y: 107
starHUD	X: 78 , Y: 69	X: 128, Y: 128
pausedbuttonHUD	X: 582, Y: 58	X: 96 , Y: 93

The food images and the bomb image need to be outside the layout. These include the cupcake, starcookie, donut, and poptart.

Main Player Animation Import

If you look inside the Hunger Croc asset "alligator" folder, you will see many animations of the main alligator player. This is how we import the animations.

1. Make sure that the current layer is set to "GAME".
2. Double-click on the layout and then select "Sprite" from the "Insert New Object" window.

We want to create three animations (idle, walk, and eat). On the animations window, right-click, and then add animations and set the name for each animation name I listed. For the walk animation, we need to import more than one image. On the "Animation Frames" window, right-click on "Import frames" and then click on "From files".. From there, you can select all the files you need. For the animation properties set the "Speed" to 8, Set Loop to No (which means the animation will not loop), Set repeat count to 1, as this will go back to animation frame 1 after the animation completes and set Ping-pong to 0 under the animation properties window.

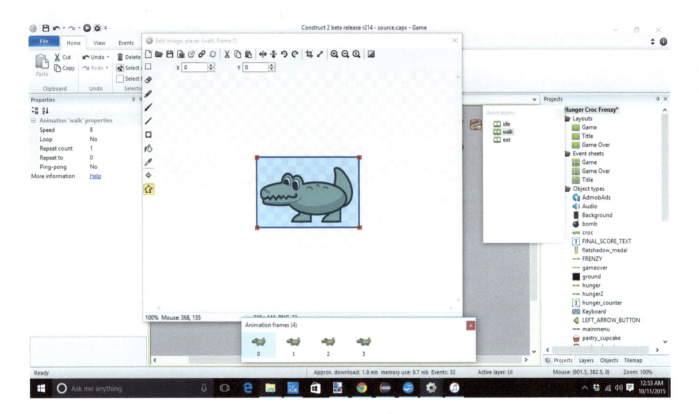

Now we need to create one more game layout called "Game Over".

With the Game Over layout currently open and the asset pack folder opened, drag the following images on the layout.

gameover.png

mainmenu.png

score.png

Resize and position them at the following values.

	Position	Size
gameover	X: 298 , Y: 148	X: 366 ,Y: 77
mainmenu	X: 324 , Y: 713	X: 476 ,Y: 82
score	X: 317, Y: 251	X: 220 ,Y: 81

Remember earlier we had to set out collision points on our touch buttons such as the "Play" button? You will need to do the same for the "Main Menu" button. Make sure it's set as a perfect rectangle. Delete extra points if you have to.

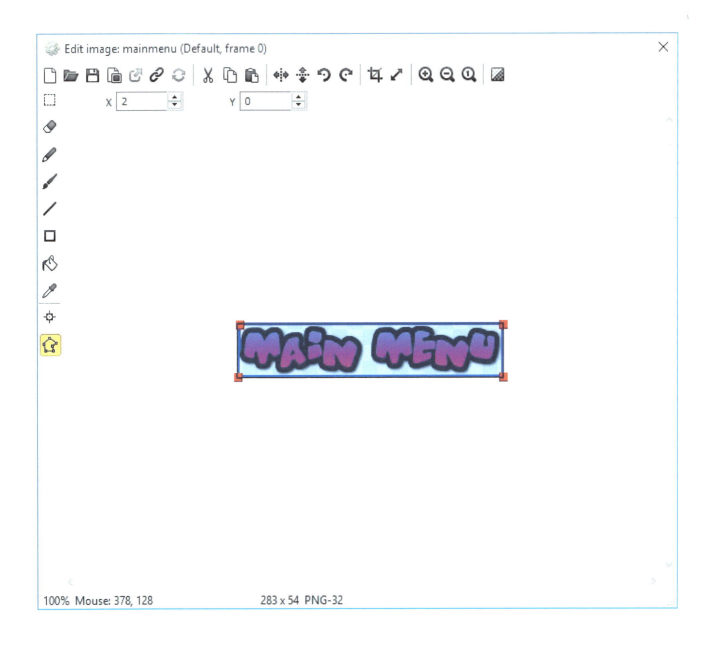

Now you will need to create a text object. This object will be used to display the score once the game is over. Name this object as "FINAL_SCORE_TEXT". Look at the images below to learn how to do this.

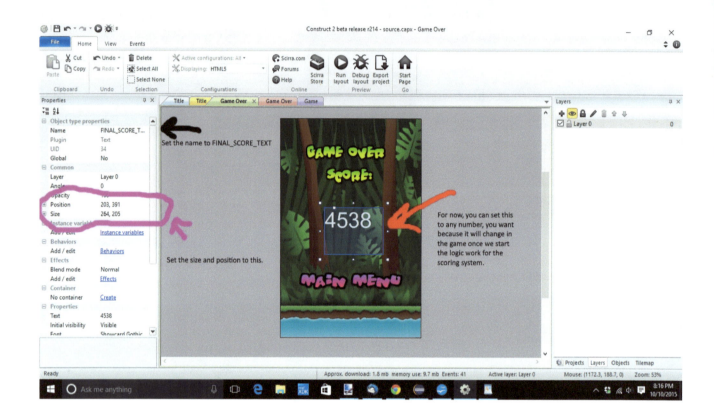

You should now have three layouts which make your game. "Title" for our main menu screen. "Game" for our main gameplay screen and "Game Over" for our game over screen once the player runs out of time. In the next section, we will be connecting the pieces together with events.

Gameplay Events

Let's begin by opening up the "Game" event sheet from our Project Bar. We will need to add two global numbers. These numbers are stored for every layout that we have in our project. To add global variables, right-click on the event sheet and select "Add Global Variable". Add

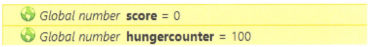

"score" with a type of "Number and a value of 0". Add "hungercounter" with a type of "Number and a value of 0."

Before we continue with our events. You need to learn about this great feature of Construct 2 called "Families." Families are basically a group of object types. Think of families as a refrigerator, inside you have different types of foods in it. Everything in the fridge is doing one thing - Trying to stay cold. Families make writing events faster and easier, because instead of writing events for each object that does the same thing. We can group together the objects and then write the logic for that one single family group.

To make a family for this project, make sure that the project bar is open. Scroll down until you see a folder that says "Families." Right-Click and select "Add Family". Now we want to select all the 4 foods in our project and then name our family as "Food."

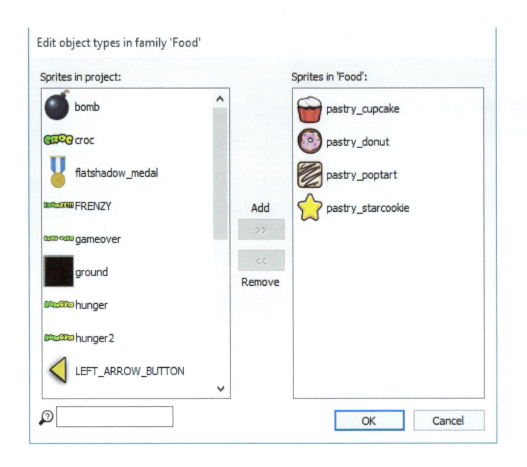

Now let's go back to the "Game" event sheet. Right-Click on the event sheet and select "Add Group." Type in "Destroy Objects After leaving screen." I use groups to tidy up my event coding, so that I know what does what. Once done, Click on "Add Event,"then select "Food" family from the "Add Event" window. Select "Compare Y".

In the next window, select "Greater than" from the Comparison drop-down menu. In the Y-Coordinate box, type in "980." Hit Done. Now click on "Add Action." Select family from the "Add Action" window. Now select "Destroy." Now drag that whole event block inside the "Destroy Objects after leaving screen" group.

Destroy Objects after leaving screen

Food	Y > 980	Food	Destroy

If we were to read what we just added as a sentence, it would say, "If any object in the Food Family is greater than 980, then delete the object." Remember that our Window Size is set at (640,960). Anything past 960 on the Y-axis, we won't technically see on the screen. So, we destroy any of the food objects that go past 980 and destroy them. We do this to preventing the game from slowing down and using too much memory.

Let's continue with the event sheet. Right-Click and Create a New Group called "Snack Generation."

<u>Next Steps:</u>
- Click "Add Event"
- Click System, Click "Every X Seconds"
- In the text box, type in int(random(1,4)) int() converts a float(fractional number ¼ or 0.25) number or text into an integer (whole
- numbers). Random (number1,number2), basically picks a number between number1 and number2. In this case, we want to find a random number between 1 and 4.
- Click "Add Action", Click "System" and then select "Create Object" and then set the following values as shown in the image below.

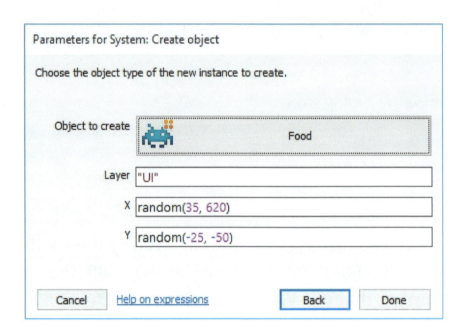

Here we want to create the food object on the UI layer. X and Y are the coordinates we want to create our object. We want our food objects to spawn in different areas of the screen, so we use "random()"again. Don't forget our main window resolution of 640,960. Notice that our Y values here are negative numbers.

This means that our food object will start spawning above the screen and it won't show yet until we start making it move, which I will discuss how to do later.
Now select that block of code, select Copy
and then Paste. You can replace this event with values for the bomb. In the end, your event code should look like this.

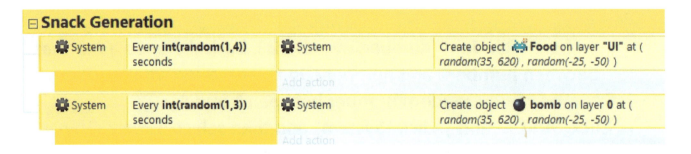

Touch Functionality

It would be nice to add some kind of controls to our alligator right? Adding controls to our games add great level of user interaction between the player and the game. Let's begin by clicking our player sprite and adding the "Platform" and "BoundtoLayout" behaviors to it. Platform behavior will give the alligator basic platform movement and the "BoundtoLayout" will make the player unable to go off-screen. Check out the image below on how to add behaviors.

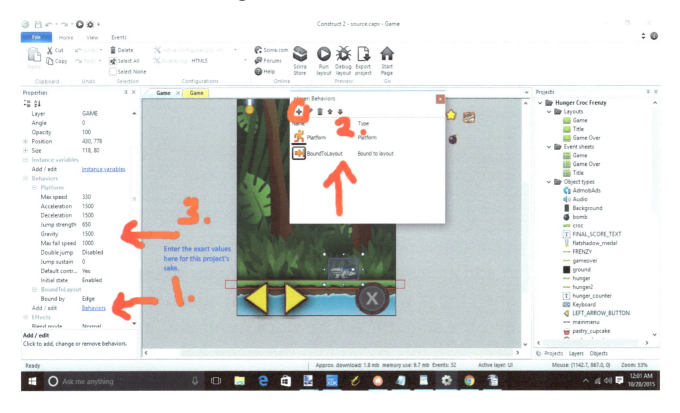

Now we need to create a new group called "Controls." We will add all of our Touch based events to this group for easy access. Inside the group, enter the following events.

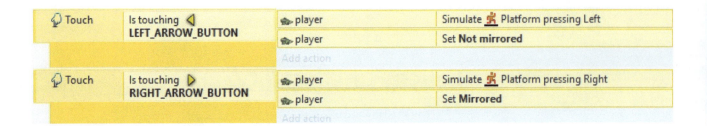

the following set of code, which checks to see when the player is touching the following buttons.
For example, If the player is touching the left arrow button, then the player sprite will move to the left. If the player is touching the right arrow button, then the player sprite will move to the right. Very simple right?

Next we need to create an event for the alligator to open it's mouth when the big X button is held. You can do so by adding the event below.

Now we need to add an event that tells the alligator to return back to idle animation when the player isn't pressing any touch buttons on the screen. Without this, the alligator will be stuck using the "eat" animation. You can do this by adding the event below.

Collision Detection

We must give our alligator, food and bomb objects collision detection in order for interaction between our objects. Without collision detection, our objects would just pass through each other with no interaction whatsoever. Create a new group called "Collisions" and add the following events inside the group:

⊟ **Collisions**			
➡ 📟 Food	On collision with 🐊 **player**	📟 Food	Destroy
🐊 player	Is animation "eat" playing	⚙ System	Add *1* to **hungercounter**
		⚙ System	Add *int(random(2,9))* to **score**
		🔊 Audio	Play **coin** not looping at volume 0 dB (tag "")
➡ ⚫ bomb	On collision with 🐊 **player**	⚫ bomb	Destroy
🐊 player	Is animation "eat" playing	⚙ System	Subtract *5* from **hungercounter**
		⚙ System	Subtract *int(random(10,25))* from **score**
		🔊 Audio	Play **a1_07133** not looping at volume 0 dB (tag "")

The events read as follows:
If any of the food objects inside "Food" family collides with the player when the player's animation "eat" is playing, then we need to destroy that food object. Add one to our hungercounter (timer). Add a random number between 2 and 9 to our main score and lastly play the "coin" sound.

We also need to create a collision event for the bomb colliding with the player. When the bomb touches the player, we need to subtract both from both the hungercounter timer and the player's score. A sound is also played when the bomb touches the player as well.

UI Text Updates

We must update our player with some type of UI. User Interfaces can be graphical, or we can use basic text as our interface. For this project, we will be using text based UI to simplify this project.

Remember our two global variables "hunger_counter" and "score_counter?" We will make these show variables on the screen and update them during our gameplay.

Begin by creating a group called "Text Updates." Now, we need create two events to tell our two global variables to update the "hunger_counter" and "score_counter" text objects.

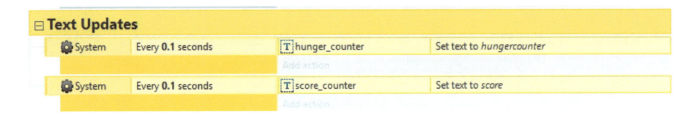

Game Over events

We need to make one more event sheet titled "Game Over." Make sure that the "Game Over" layout is linked to the "Game Over" event sheet as shown on the image below.

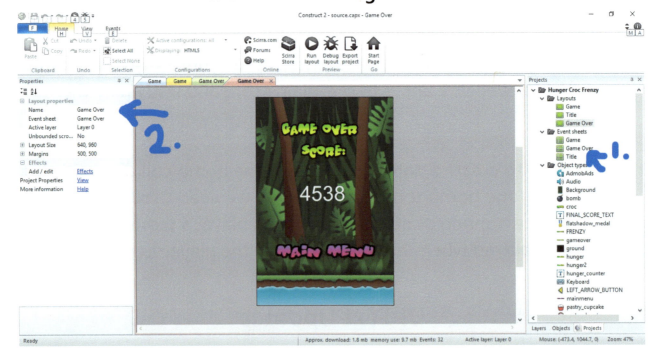

With the "Game Over" event sheet open, we begin by adding a Global number called submitscore and we want it to equal 1.

Global number **submitscore** = 1

Before we continue in our event sheet, we need to add the "Admob"
object into our project.
Go to any of the layouts that you may have open and double-click
outside the layout. Select the "Admob" object. Admob is used to
monetize our games with ads. We will talk more about how to utilize
Admob in our project in a few.

Back into the "Game Over" event sheet, begin by inserting the following
events.

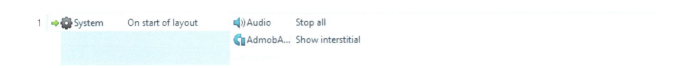

This tells us when the "Game Over" screen shows, stop all the audio
that's currently playing and show an Admob Interstitial (Full Screen) ad.
Now enter the following events below.

This set of events tells us that when the Main Menu button is touched, that we need to set the score to 0, set the hungercounter timer back to 100 and we need to have the player to return back to the "Title" screen which is the main menu.

Our last event that we need to add to finish up our "Game Over" event sheet is that we need to update our FINAL_SCORE_TEXT UI every tick.

Final touches

Our game is almost complete, so we need to go ahead and add the last few events needed. Go back to the "Game" event sheet and add the last few events.

18	System	Every 0.7 seconds	System	Subtract 1 from **hungercounter**
19	System	**hungercounter** ≥ 100	System	Set **hungercounter** to 100
20	System	On start of layout	Audio	Play 350235_Oscar_Remius__Sexy looping at volume 0 dB (tag "")
21	System	**hungercounter** ≤ 0	System	Go to **Game Over**
22	Touch	On touched **pause_hud**	Pause	Toggle pause
23	Pause	On pause	paused	Set Visible
24	Pause	On resume	paused	Set Invisible

Here's what the last few events mean.

1.) **Every 0.7 seconds, we will subtract 1 from our hungercounter timer.**

2.) **To prevent the hungercounter timer from going over 100, we set it a cap of 100.**

3.) **On the start of the layout, we want to play our main game music with a volume of 0 db (decibels).**

4.) **If our hungercounter timer is equal or less than 0, then we need to make our player go to the "Game Over" Screen.**

5.) **If the player touches on the "pause_hud" object, then we need to toggle pause from Rex's Pause Plugin.**

6.) **If the pause plugin is running active on pause, then we need to set the "Paused" UI to visible.**

7.) **If the pause plugin isn't active on pausing, then we need to set the "Paused" UI to Invisible.**

Admob Ads

In order to monetize free apps, we will need to implement the Admob plugin into our game which we already have. Earlier, we added in an event to show Admob Interstitial (Full Screen) ads, but they won't show on the mobile device until we create what's called an Interstitial ID.

Steps:

1.) Register for Admob.com account.

2.) After logging into Admob, click on **"Monetize New App"**.

3.) Click on **"Add your app manually"**.

4.) Type in "**Hunger Croc Frenzy**" in the text box.

5.) Don't worry about adding in Analytics if it asks you. Select "Interstitial" for the ad format. Give it a name and then copy and paste into the Interstitial textbox inside your project.

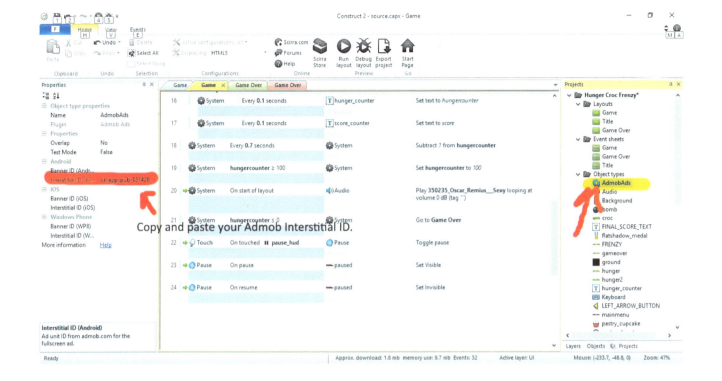

Exporting your game

It's time to export our game to Intel XDK. Intel XDK is a tool that converts HTML5 games into many formats such as iOS, Android, Windows Phone and more! We will export our project into Cordova. Cordova is a platform used to build HTML5 applications to iOS, Android, and many other platforms. Go to ==File > Export Project > Select Cordova.== Save the export to a folder for easy access.

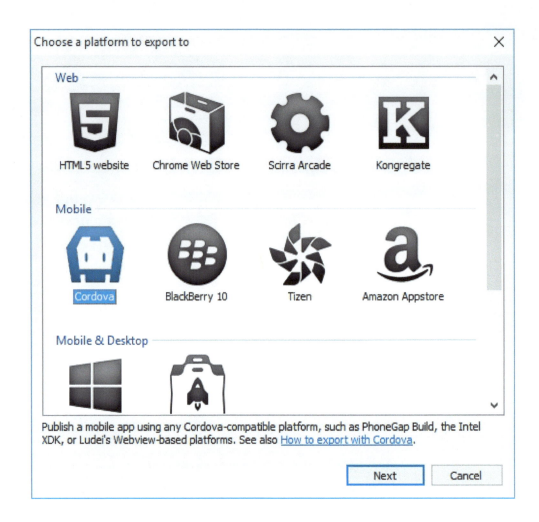

Intel XDK

Download Intel XDK:

https://software.intel.com/en-us/intel-xdk

Once installed, it's time to import our project. Click on <mark>"Start New Project" then click on "Import Your Code Base."</mark> You will need to select the directory location where you have exported your Cordova HTML5 project files. After you selected the directory, go ahead and enter your project name. In this case it would be labelled "Hunger Croc Frenzy." Hit Ok, and then make sure <mark>"Use Cordova Plugins"</mark> is set to <mark>"Yes"</mark>. This is needed for the Admob Plugin to work for our game. After the game has imported, click on "XDK Projects" icon. Turn off the following icons as shown below by clicking on them. This will disable certain platforms we don't want to publish our game on.

These are the platform buttons such as Android, Android(Crosswalk), iOS, and Windows Phone 8.

Select <mark>Plugin Management</mark>, Click the <mark>"Add Plugins to this Project."</mark> <mark>Select Featured Plugins</mark> > then select <mark>Admob* Ad Services (CLI5)</mark> (As of Intel XDK Build 2673) <mark>If you have an older version of Intel XDK, then it should marked as Admob Ad Services (old)</mark>.

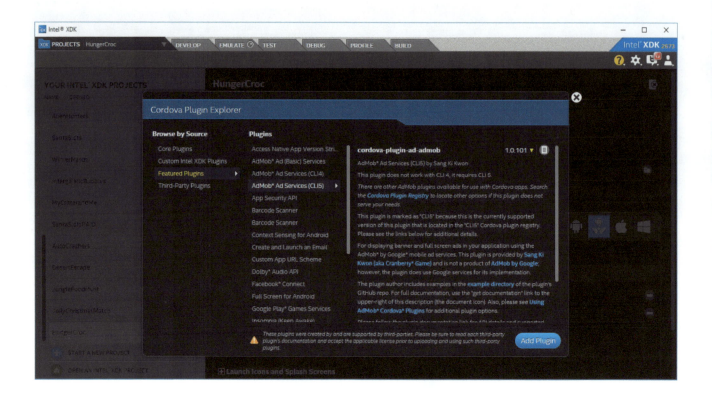

Click on "Build Settings" and enter the following info.

APP ID: com.companyname.hungercrocfrenzy (Make sure to replace the company name with your own company name.)

APP Name: Hunger Croc Frenzy

Author: (Your Company Name)

APP Version: 1.0

Fullscreen: Checked

Orientation: Portrait

APP Version Code: 1 (You will need to increment this number by one everytime you roll out a new game update on Google Play)

Finally, we need to add our app icons to our Intel XDK project. Look inside your asset pack and you will see 4 sets of icons labelled "icon_36.png, icon_48.png, icon_72.png and icon_96.png". These are different sizes icons for mobile phones and tablets of different sizes. The bigger resolution on your phone or tablet, then the bigger the app icon will show on the screen. Drag these four icons from the asset pack folder to your Cordova export folder. These icons have to be in the same directory where your Intel XDK project files are located.

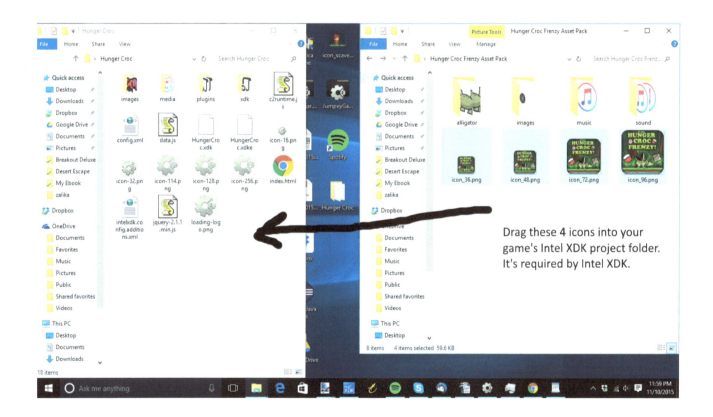

Final Testing and Android APK Creation

To test and see how our game will look on a mobile phone, click on the "Emulate" tab. On this screen, you will be able to test the game on different phone sizes. Please note that emulation doesn't equate to a mobile device's actual speed. For example, the app might run fast on emulation, but if a mobile device is naturally slow, then it will run this game slow.

Now we are ready to export our game to .APK format which is an Android Application Package files which will install our game to all kinds of mobile devices. Click on the Build tab, then click under "Crosswalk for Android" click on "Build."

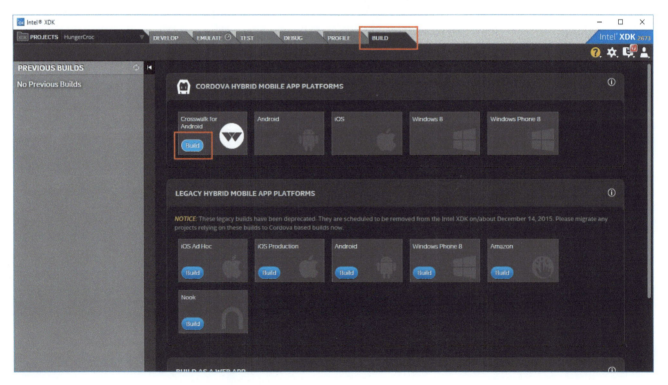

Within a few minutes, you will have an APK that you can download to submit to the Google Play Developer Console. Just make sure that you have a developer account. There's a one-time cost of $25 dollars to register for a Google Play Developer Account. When uploading the APK, it's best to upload the ARM version, because 95% of the devices in the market are using these type of CPUs. The x86 (Intel) based mobile devices simply are not that popular.

Congratulations! I hope you learned a lot for this book. Please note that this is only the beginning of creating Android games. Construct 2 really simplifies the process and you will be on your way to creating many games and making decent profit. I wish you the best of luck!

If you would like to get in touch with me, you can follow me on Twitter. My twitter handle is @jettas88.

BONUS: How to advertise your game for downloads.

Now that you've learned how to make an Android game, but what if you're clueless on how to advertise your game to actual make money? Well, I'm here to help you out. The rest of this guide will assume that you have little to no budget for promoting your games and apps.

Facebook Groups

Popular Facebook Groups can help your app gain exposure believe it or not. Some groups have rules for posting, so make sure you view those rules first. I've compiled a list of some of the best Facebook Groups you can use to advertise your games.

Largest Facebook Group Ever: https://www.facebook.com/groups/ohyaaaa/
Promote yourself worldwide: https://www.facebook.com/groups/326500524097768/
Indie Game Promo: https://www.facebook.com/groups/227592780726252/
Biggest Advertising Group: https://www.facebook.com/groups/makeitbiggest/
Promote your skills/talents/jobs, etc:
https://www.facebook.com/groups/209323502483381/
Free Mobile Games Advertising Hub:
https://www.facebook.com/groups/freegameads/

You can also advertise on websites like Craigslist, reddit, Twitter and Facebook to advertise your own game for free. If you want to spend a little bit of money, then you can use Facebook Ads, Fiverr or simply pay for a review of your game. The link below includes a massive list of some of the best review sites for Apple and Android.

Best App Review Sites:
https://docs.google.com/spreadsheet/ccc?key=0AvcBksh1GeWHdHQ1ek1Uc3JUNk5oLWV

ASO

App Store Optimization is the ability to help developers promote their apps by improving the visibility of their app. In order to gain decent downloads, you must rank higher than your competitors of the game concept by specific keywords in your app description. When starting off with your app, you must choose relevant keywords that matches your app's genre. For example, if your game consists of zombie survival, then keywords like "zombie, survival, dead, gore, blood, etc. Luckily, you don't have to manually come up with words to help your app gain exposures. There's several sites that you can visit and try out each site as they can give you different results. Here's my favorite websites..

ASO Research Websites:

Straply: http://www.straply.com
Sensortower: http://www.sensortower.com
MobileDevHQ: http://www.mobiledevhq.com
SearchMan: http://www.searchman.com

Credits

Ashley Gullen – Founder of Construct 2
Daniel Newbanks – Book Edits
Vicki Wenderlich – Asset Graphics
rexrainbow from Scirra Forums – Rex's Pause Plugin
Maverlyn from Newgrounds.com - Music

www.ingramcontent.com/pod-product-compliance
Lightning Source LLC
Chambersburg PA
CBHW050937060326
40689CB00040B/645